CYNTHIA ERIVO:

A Life in Music, Theater, and Film-The Unstoppable Journey of a Modern Icon

Justin M. Eaton

Cynthia Erivo

Copyright Page

The Origins and Cultural Impacts

Copyright © 2024 by Justin M. Eaton

All rights reserved. No part of this publication may be reproduced, distributed, or transmitted in any form or by any means, including photocopying, recording, or other electronic or mechanical methods, without the prior written permission of the publisher, except in the case of brief quotations embodied in critical reviews and certain other noncommercial uses permitted by copyright law. For permission requests, write to the publisher at the address below.

Cynthia Erivo

Printed in united state

Library of Congress Cataloging-in-Publication Data [Include if relevant, or replace with a placeholder if unknown]

This book is a work of nonfiction. While the author has made every effort to ensure the accuracy of the information herein, the publisher assumes no responsibility for errors or omissions.

This format can be customized with specific publisher and author details.

TABLE OF CONTENT

INTRODUCTION

CHAPTER 1: WHO IS CYNTHIA ERIVO

1.1 Early life

1.2 Background

CHAPTER 2: THEATER CAREER

2.1 Breakthrough Role: The Color Purple

2.2 Other Notable Stage Performances

2.3 Plauded Musical Exhibitions

CHAPTER 3:FILM AND TELEVISION CAREER

3.1 Important Television Positions

3.2 Upcoming Projects

CHAPTER 4:MUSICAL CAREER

4.1 Historical Musical Inspirations

4.2 Broadway Achievement

4.3 Career in Solo Music

4.4 Live Performances and Concerts

4.5 Music as Social Change

4.6 Grammy Awards Won

4.7 Other Music-Related Achievements

CHAPTER 5: ACTIVISM

5.1 Social Justice Advocacy

5.2 Mental Health Advocacy

5.3 In favor of LGBTQ+ Rights

5.4 Charitable Work

5.5 Using Art for Social Change

5.6 Speaking in Public and Involvement

CHAPTER 6: AWARDS AND RECOGNITIONS

6.1 The following information relates to her Academy Award nominations:

6.2. Stand Up (2020) - Best Original Song

6.3 Outstanding Accomplishments Associated with the Nominations

CHAPTER 7: STYLE

7.1. Aesthetic of Fashion

7.2. Red Carpet Looks

7.3. Costume for Performance

7. 4. Hair and Makeup

7.5 Individual Expression

7.6 Impact

7.7. Arts and Cultural Representation

7.8 Empowerment via Music

7.9 Cultural Impact

7.10 Fashion Influence

7.11 Social Media Engagement

7.12 Motivational Leader

CHAPTER 8:FUTURE PROJECTS AND ENDEAVORS

8.1 New Film Initiatives

8.2 Future Projects in Theater

8.3. Future Musical Initiatives

8.4 Additional Creative Projects

8.5 Potential production and directing roles

8.6 Directorial Projects

8.7 Manufacturing Activities

8.8 Emphasis Areas and Themes

8.9 Possible Partnerships

CONCLUSION

Cynthia Erivo

INTRODUCTION

Cynthia Erivo is a power of nature, a solitary ability that has spellbound crowds across various mediums. Brought into the world in London to Nigerian settlers, Erivo has quickly arisen as one of the most adaptable and convincing entertainers of her age. With her taking off voice, directing stage presence, and capacity to channel profound inclination, she has made a permanent imprint on theater, music, and movies.

This book chronicles her journey from a young child with lofty aspirations to a global phenomenon, acclaimed for her Broadway shows, Grammy-winning songs, and powerful on-screen personas. From her groundbreaking role as Celie in *The Variety Purple*, which earned her a Tony Grant, to her highly acclaimed portrayal of Harriet Tubman in *Harriet*, which earned her a Brilliant Globe and a Foundation Grant, Cynthia Erivo's career is an exemplar of perseverance, talent, and unwavering faith in one's abilities.

Beyond her artistic achievements, Cynthia has become a positive role model for some thanks to her advocacy for diversity, representation, and civil rights. Her energy, reason, and credibility resonate with people all over the world, whether she is in front of the camera, on the show stage, or the honorary pathway.

In this book, we explore many aspects of Cynthia Erivo's life and career, including her rise to prominence, her

Cynthia Erivo

inventive style, and her lasting influence on media outlets. Cynthia Erivo: A Day-to-Day Life in Music, Theater, and Film honors her remarkable journey and the legacy she is working as a cutting-edge symbol through interviews, execution examination, and a more critical look at the woman behind the jobs.

CHAPTER 1: WHO IS CYNTHIA ERIVO

Cynthia Erivo is a British actress, singer, and songwriter known for her remarkable talent across multiple art forms, including theater, film, and music. Born on January 8, 1987, in London, Erivo rose to fame with her Tony Award-winning performance as Celie in the 2015 Broadway revival of *The Color Purple*. Her powerful voice and emotional depth in the role made her a standout in the theater world, and she also earned a

Cynthia Erivo

Grammy Award and a Daytime Emmy for her work in the production.

Erivo leaped theater to the big screen, starring in movies like *Bad Times at the El Royale* (2018), *Widows* (2018), and, most notably, *Harriet* (2019) as Harriet Tubman. She was nominated for a Golden Globe and an Academy Award for her portrayal of the renowned abolitionist. In addition to her work in acting, Cynthia Erivo is a gifted vocalist who has participated in several musical projects and released music.

In addition to her artistic accomplishments, Erivo is well-known for her advocacy and activism, especially about issues of diversity and representation in the entertainment business. As she takes on new roles in advocacy, music, and acting, her career keeps developing, making her one of the most dynamic and significant performers of her generation.

1.1 Early life

On January 8, 1987, Cynthia Erivo was born in Stockwell, South London, to parents who were immigrants from Nigeria. Erivo was raised by a single mother who was a nurse and lived in a mixed-race working-class neighborhood. She demonstrated a great love of the arts, particularly music, at a young age, displaying early indications of the extraordinary talent that would later define her career.

Cynthia Erivo

Her love of performing took off while she was a student at La Retraite Roman Catholic Girls' School in Clapham, a Catholic all-girls school. Erivo began training in drama shortly after her teachers encouraged her to follow her artistic interests. At the University of East London, she first majored in psychology before realizing performance was her true calling. After realizing this, she decided to enroll in one of the most prominent acting programs in the world, the Royal Academy of Dramatic Art (RADA).

Erivo developed her talents while attending RADA, obtaining the technical instruction that would later form the basis of her acting and singing careers. Her ability to handle challenging roles and give strong performances on stage and screen was shaped by her classical training.

Erivo attributes her career's discipline and drive to her early upbringing, and she gives her mother credit for instilling in her the belief that persistence and hard work could lead her to her goals.

Erivo's early years shaped her into the adaptable and dynamic performer she is today, paving the way for her breakthrough roles and international recognition.

1.2 Background

Cynthia Erivo's upbringing in London and her Nigerian ancestry play a significant role in shaping her identity and artistic sensibilities. Her mother, a nurse, raised her after her parents immigrated from Nigeria to South

Cynthia Erivo

London, where she was born. Her upbringing in both British and Nigerian customs gave her a strong sense of identity and resilience, and her cultural background played a significant role in her early years.

Erivo's exposure to a variety of cultures and experiences during her upbringing in the multicultural neighborhood of Stockwell, London, deepened her perspective on the world. She learned the virtues of perseverance, hard effort, and self-belief from her mother and this environment. Cynthia didn't grow up surrounded by theater or the arts, but she did discover early on that she loved performing, especially when it came to acting and music, which she studied in school.

Cynthia Erivo

She attended La Retraite Roman Catholic Girls' School for her first education, and then the University of East London where she completed her psychology degree. Erivo, however, quickly changed course after realizing that the performing arts were her true calling. After that, she received her training at one of the world's most prestigious drama schools, the Royal Academy of Dramatic Art (RADA). She honed the discipline and skill that would launch her career at RADA.

The combination of Nigerian culture, British upbringing, and formal theatrical training that made up Cynthia Erivo's background has had a significant impact on her work. Her performances, on stage or screen, often touch on themes of identity, struggle, and triumph because of the distinct perspective it has given her.

CHAPTER 2: THEATER CAREER

Through her incredible career in theater, Cynthia Erivo has demonstrated her exceptional talent and adaptability as a performer. Her training at the Royal Academy of Dramatic Art (RADA), where she honed her craft and got ready for a career on stage, was the first step in her ascent in the theater industry.

2.1 Breakthrough Role: The Color Purple

Cynthia Erivo

Erivo's big break came in 2015 when she was chosen to play Celie in the Broadway production of *The Color Purple*, the musical adaptation of the critically acclaimed novel by Alice Walker. She received a great deal of praise for her intense and moving performance, and she soon established herself as a notable star. Erivo's performance of "I'm Here" left a lasting impression on the audience and demonstrated both her extraordinary acting and vocal skills. She received numerous honors for the role, including a Daytime Emmy Award for her performance in the musical's live broadcast, a Tony Award for Best Actress in a Musical, and a Grammy Award for Best Musical Theater Album.

2.2 Other Notable Stage Performances

After her triumph in *The Color Purple*, Erivo kept accepting difficult and varied roles in the theater. She made appearances in several shows, such as:

1. The Umbrellas of Cherbourg: Erivo portrayed Geneviève in this musical, which has music by Michel Legrand. Her ability to deliver breathtaking musical numbers while navigating difficult emotional landscapes was on full display during her performance.

2. A London production of The Color Purple
She starred in the critically acclaimed London production of *The Color Purple* in 2013, prior to her

Broadway success. She became known as a formidable talent in the theater world thanks to this performance.

2.3 Plauded Musical Exhibitions

Erivo has shown versatility as a vocalist by participating in a variety of concert performances and special events, in addition to performing on stage. She has collaborated with well-known performers and appeared in prestigious settings, which has enhanced her standing as a captivating performer.

2.4 Effect on the Community of Theater

Beyond her stage appearances, Cynthia Erivo has a lasting influence on the theater community. Being a woman of color in a field that is dominated by white people, she has emerged as a spokesperson for representation and diversity in the arts. Many would-be actors, especially young women of color, have been encouraged to follow their dreams of becoming theater professionals by her success.

CHAPTER 3: FILM AND TELEVISION CAREER

Through her work on television, Cynthia Erivo has demonstrated her range as an actress and her capacity to hold the attention of viewers in a variety of genres. Her strong performances and dedication to storytelling have distinguished her move from theater and film to television. The following are some of her television career's major highlights:

3.1 Important Television Positions

1. The Outsider (2020): Erivo portrayed Holly Gibney, a private investigator with a distinct viewpoint, in this HBO miniseries based on Stephen King's book. Her performance received recognition for its richness and depth, showcasing her capacity to give a character

dealing with unusual circumstances depth. Positive reviews were given to the show, which showcased Erivo's dramatic role-playing skills.

2. The Color Purple: 2023 (CBS): Erivo reprised her beloved role as Celie from the Broadway revival as she starred in the CBS live concert production of *The Color Purple*. Her emotional range and amazing vocal abilities were on display during the performance, which strengthened her bond with the role and the musical.

3. Genius: Aretha (2021): Erivo played the renowned singer Aretha Franklin in the National Geographic anthology series. Her ability to sing was demonstrated in this role, as she sang several of Franklin's well-known songs throughout the show. Erivo was nominated for a

Primetime Emmy Award for Outstanding Lead Actress in a Limited Series or Movie as a result of her critically acclaimed performance.

3.2 Upcoming Projects

Cynthia Erivo is set to appear in several upcoming television projects that continue to showcase her range and talent. Her involvement in new series and collaborations with established creators promises to further her impact on the medium.

1. Advocacy and Representation:
Erivo's presence on television extends beyond her performances; she is also an advocate for diversity and

representation in the industry. By taking on significant roles in high-profile projects, she helps to challenge stereotypes and open doors for other actors of color in television.

Cynthia Erivo's television career is a testament to both her commitment to powerful storytelling and her remarkable range as an actress. She keeps leaving a lasting impression on television with her captivating performances and dedication to representation, enthralling viewers and motivating upcoming performers. Her impact on television is probably only going to increase as she takes on more roles and endeavors, solidifying her status as a major player in the entertainment business.

CHAPTER 4: MUSICAL CAREER

Cynthia Erivo's impressive vocal prowess and knack for connecting with listeners via song are demonstrated by her successful musical career. Her musical career has been distinguished by her versatility, emotion, and unwavering dedication to her craft, starting from her theater roots and continuing through her successes in recording and live performances. Here are a few of her musical career's major highlights:

4.1 Historical Musical Inspirations

Cynthia Erivo

Erivo grew up surrounded by music, and the rich cultural sounds and rhythms of her Nigerian background serve as a rich background. She sang in church a lot, which helped her voice become more beautiful, and her love of acting and music grew together. This basis cleared the path for her subsequent musical pursuits.

4.2 Broadway Achievement

With her role in *The Color Purple*, Cynthia Erivo not only demonstrated her acting prowess but also her remarkable singing voice, which launched her career. Her performance of stirring songs like "I'm Here" enthralled both critics and audiences, earning her multiple honors, including a Grammy Award for Best

Cynthia Erivo

Musical Theater Album for the cast recording of the production.

4.3 Career in Solo Music

After experiencing success on Broadway, Erivo started to look into pursuing a solo music career. She has several singles and albums that demonstrate her versatility in pop, R&B, and soul music. Among her well-known musical compositions are:

1. Stand Up : She co-wrote this original song for the movie *Harriet*, demonstrating her ability to write stirring anthems. She was nominated for a Grammy Award and an Academy Award for Best Original Song for the song. Listeners are moved by its message of

empowerment and resiliency, which highlights Erivo's dedication to using her music to effect change.

2. EPs and Singles: Erivo has put out a number of singles that showcase her emotional range and vocal talent. Her songs frequently incorporate pop and soul influences, and the lyrics touch on issues of empowerment, love, and identity.

4.4 Live Performances and Concerts

Erivo's recorded work, in addition to her performances at various prestigious events and venues, has further solidified her reputation as a talented vocalist. Whether she is performing classics or original music, her ability to enthrall audiences is evident in her concert performances.

4.5 Music as Social Change

With her platform, Cynthia Erivo promotes social justice and diversity in the music business. Through her performances and songs, she calls attention to important issues and inspires her audience to take action. Her songs frequently discuss both her personal experiences and the more significant problems that marginalized communities face.

- Cynthia Erivo's accomplishments in the music business are evidence of her exceptional talent and commitment to her craft. Here are a few of her most noteworthy achievements in the music industry, including her Grammy victory and other noteworthy honors:

4.6 Grammy Awards Won

1. Best Musical Theater Album Grammy Award (2017)

For: Broadway Revival Cast Recording of The Color Purple (2015)

Importance: This Grammy victory honored the cast recording's exceptional quality, showcasing Erivo's stirring portrayal of Celie. The honor emphasized her vocal prowess on a national scale and cemented her place as a notable personality in the musical theater industry.

Cynthia Erivo

4.7 Other Music-Related Achievements:

1. Academy Award Nominations: Harriet (2020) for Best Actress: For her portrayal of Harriet Tubman, Erivo, who is talented in both acting and music, was nominated for an Oscar.

Harriet received a nomination for Best Original Song for "Stand Up" (2020) because of the song's strong message and poignant effect.

2. Golden Globe Nominations: Harriet (2020) for Best Actress in a Motion Picture – Drama: This nomination resulted from the praise that her performance received from critics.

Cynthia Erivo

Best Original Song for "Stand Up" (2020): The song, which highlights empowerment and resiliency, receives additional recognition.

3. Genius: Aretha (2021): Outstanding Lead Actress in a Limited Series or Movie is the subject of a Primetime Emmy nomination. Erivo received great appreciation for her portrayal of Aretha Franklin, and her outstanding work earned her an Emmy nomination.

4. BET Award for Best Actress (2020): This honor highlights her influence as an actress and musician and acknowledges her exceptional performance in *Harriet*.

5. MTV Movie & TV Awards: **Harriet* (2020)**'s Best Breakthrough Performance: This award recognized

her as a rising star in the industry and highlighted her remarkable transition from theater to film.

6. NAACP Image Awards: *Harriet* (2020)** for Outstanding Actress in a Motion Picture Erivo's impressive performance in this part won her praise, enhancing her reputation as a gifted actress.

7. BBC Radio 2 Concert Performance: Erivo has given live performances on several esteemed occasions, such as the BBC Radio 2 concert series, where she showcased her vocal abilities to a broader audience and garnered further recognition.

8. Live Performances: Erivo has given stirring performances at important occasions, such as the

Academy Awards, where she sang "Stand Up" with passion, solidifying her standing as a formidable live vocalist.

CHAPTER 5: ACTIVISM

In addition to her artistic accomplishments, Cynthia Erivo is praised for her dedication to social justice and activism. She utilizes her position as a well-known person in the entertainment sector to promote change and increase awareness of different issues. Here are a few salient features of her activism:

5.1 Social Justice Advocacy

1. Racial Equality: Erivo has used her platform to confront systemic racism and injustice, and she has been a strong voice for racial equality. She frequently expresses her opinions about the value of diversity in all fields and the importance of representation in the arts on social media and in interviews.
2. Support for the Black Lives Matter Movement: Erivo actively participated in demonstrations and used her voice to advocate for the Black Lives Matter movement following the murder of George Floyd and the ensuing protests in 2020. She underlined how critical it is to speak out against discrimination and acts of racial violence.

3. Empowerment of Marginalized Voices: Women and people of color in particular are among the marginalized communities that Erivo is committed to elevating. She wants to tell stories that highlight the experiences of these communities and strike a chord with them through her work in theater, film, and music.

5.2 Mental Health Advocacy

Erivo has been transparent about the significance of mental health, especially for Black people. She highlights the need to address mental health issues, lowering stigma, and enticing people to get support.

5.3 In favor of LGBTQ+ Rights

As an ally of the LGBTQ+ community, Cynthia Erivo has promoted LGBTQ+ visibility and rights through her platform. She has participated in activities that support equality and acceptance for all people, regardless of their sexual orientation or gender identity, and she has spoken out against discrimination.

5.4 Charitable Work

Erivo has supported organizations that prioritize social justice, health, and education through a variety of charitable endeavors. She frequently donates her time and voice to campaigns and fundraising events that try to improve communities.

Cynthia Erivo

5.5 Using Art for Social Change

Erivo works in theater, film, and music and aims to spread awareness of social issues. Songs like *Harriet*'s"StandUp" are calls to action that inspire listeners to fight for justice and equality in addition to being anthems of empowerment.

5.6 Speaking in Public and Involvement

Erivo takes part in talks, panels, and interviews where she discusses significant social issues and pushes for reform. She converses with audiences about the value of diversity in the arts and the necessity of structural social change.

Cynthia Erivo's identity as an artist is inextricably linked to her activism. She encourages others to take up the battle for change by using her platform to promote social justice, racial equality, and the voice of the marginalized. She continues to have a profound influence on society via her art and activism, leaving a long-lasting legacy as a gifted performer and an ardent activist.

CHAPTER 6:AWARDS AND RECOGNITIONS

For her work in movies, Cynthia Erivo has won a lot of accolades, most notably her Academy Award nominations.

6.1 The following information relates to her Academy Award nominations:

1. *Harriet* (2020) Best Actress

Part of: The biographical film *Harriet*, which recounts the tale of Tubman's valiant attempts to guide enslaved people to freedom via the Underground Railroad, stars Erivo as the renowned abolitionist Harriet Tubman.

2. Significance: Erivo was nominated for her first Academy Award in the Best Actress category. She was

able to portray Tubman's tenacity and resolve with a performance that won accolades for authenticity, depth, and emotional range.

6.2. Stand Up (2020) - Best Original Song

1. Song Context: Erivo and Joshuah Brian Campbell composed "Stand Up" especially for *Harriet*. The song embodies Tubman's struggle for justice and freedom and acts as an anthem of resiliency and empowerment.

2. Impact: Erivo's outstanding vocal performance and the song's strong message were acknowledged by the nomination for Best Original Song. "Stand Up" is a call

to action for social justice and change that embodies the film's themes and has struck a chord with viewers.

6.3 Outstanding Accomplishments Associated with the Nominations

1. Acknowledgment: Erivo's nominations for Best Original Song and Best Actress made her stand out as one of the few people to receive nominations for both songwriting and acting in the same year.

2 Cultural Impact: Her portrayal of Black stories and social justice advocacy in *Harriet* and the song "Stand Up" that goes with it have strengthened her stature as a major force in the entertainment business.

Cynthia Erivo

The Academy Award nominations Cynthia Erivo received for *Harriet* are evidence of her extraordinary skill as a songwriter and actress. Her performances serve as both a platform for her artistic talents and a means of advancing cultural discussions on issues of empowerment, history, and race.

Her influence on the film industry and other fields is probably only going to increase as she takes on more and more varied roles and projects.

CHAPTER 7: STYLE

Cynthia Erivo's style, which reflects her colorful personality and varied career, is an alluring fusion of elegance, boldness, and personal expression. The following essential elements of her style set her apart in both performance and fashion:

7.1. Aesthetic of Fashion

1. Bold Decisions: Erivo is renowned for her readiness to try out new looks. When it comes to the red carpet and public appearances, she frequently chooses statement pieces, vivid colors, and distinctive silhouettes.

2. Cultural Influence: Erivo frequently includes traditional motifs and elements in her clothing, drawing on her Nigerian ancestry. Her style gains depth from this cultural influence, which also honors her heritage.

3. High-Profile Designers: She regularly works with well-known fashion designers, presenting lines from Schiaparelli, Valentino, and Versace, among others. She stands out in the fashion industry for her confident wear of elaborate designs.

7.2. Red Carpet Looks

1. Memorable Outfits: Erivo has garnered attention on the red carpet with several noteworthy looks. Her electric blue Oscar gown, which featured an elaborate cape and intricate details, was particularly noteworthy as it demonstrated her ability to draw attention and make a statement.

2. Accentuation: She frequently accessorizes her looks with eye-catching pieces, such as striking shoes and jewelry, which elevate her overall appearance.

7.3. Costume for Performance

1. Theatricality: Erivo embraces theatrical elements in her attire during her performances, which correspond with the characters she plays. Her wardrobe choices, whether for a Broadway show or a movie, are meant to amplify her narrative.

2. Comfort Meets Style: Erivo prioritizes comfort while maintaining her distinct style, ensuring that her outfits

allow her to perform freely and expressively. This balance is crucial for her high-energy performance.

7. 4. Hair and Makeup

1. Signature Hairstyles: Erivo frequently sports a range of hairstyles, from sleek updos to natural curls, which highlight her adaptability and originality. Her hairstyles frequently go well with her clothes, completing her look.

2. Bold Makeup Choices: She usually wears makeup that accentuates her features and draws attention to them with vibrant colors and artistic designs. She embraces originality in makeup, which is consistent with her bold approach to style.

Cynthia Erivo

7.5 Individual Expression

1. Authenticity: Erivo frequently chooses items that are in line with her identity and values, so her style is a true reflection of who she is. She expresses herself through fashion, using her choices to spread messages of individuality and empowerment.

2. Advocacy Through Fashion: She occasionally uses her public appearances to advocate for change and visibility by incorporating messages about social justice and representation into her wardrobe.

Cynthia Erivo's bold decisions, cultural influences, and dedication to authenticity define her style, which is a potent extension of her artistic identity. She has become a well-known figure in the entertainment and fashion industries thanks to her fashion choices, which reflect her values and unique style whether she is performing or walking the red carpet. Erivo's ability to combine artistic expression with personal flair and her distinct sense of style never ceases to inspire others.

7.6 Impact

Beyond her successes on the stage and in the studio as an actress and singer, Cynthia Erivo is a well-known supporter of social justice and representation. Here are significant domains where her impact is especially noteworthy:

Cynthia Erivo

7.8. Arts and Cultural Representation

1. Pioneering Roles: Erivo has portrayed prominent Black stories and experiences in a number of films, such as *Harriet* (Harriet Tubman) and *Genius: Aretha* (Aretha Franklin). She draws attention to the significance of representation and the stories of marginalized communities by bringing these well-known figures to life.

2. A Source of Motivation for Future Artists: Erivo is a role model for many aspiring artists, having achieved success as a Black woman in theater and film. Her transformation from a little child in London to an

Academy Award-nominated performer inspires people to follow their passions in the face of adversity.

Second, Social Justice Advocacy

3. Speaking Up for Vital Issues: Erivo actively utilizes her platform to speak out against injustices against women, police brutality, and racial inequality. She spreads her message and inspires her audience to get involved in social activism through her involvement in movements like Black Lives Matter.

7.9 Empowerment via Music

Harriet's "StandUp" and other songs are anthems of empowerment that exhort listeners to stand up to injustice and defend their rights. Her songs encourage listeners to take up the cause of change by frequently expressing themes of optimism and resiliency.

7.10 Cultural Impact

1. Celebration of Heritage: Erivo showcases her Nigerian heritage by fusing aspects of her culture into her wardrobe and performances. It also inspires others to value their cultural heritage by promoting cultural pride.

2. Communiqués with Broader Views: Erivo's work adds to crucial discussions regarding history, race, and identity. She enlightens audiences and widens viewpoints by highlighting important Black history personalities and events.

7.11 Fashion Influence

1.Brave Fashion Selections: Erivo is renowned for her audacious and imaginative sense of style. She is a fashion icon and influencer since her distinct style frequently captures the essence of her personality and creativity. She exhorts people to embrace risk-taking and use their clothes as a means of self-expression.

2.Designer Collaborations: Erivo promotes diversity in the fashion industry and raises the profile of Black designers by working with well-known designers and exhibiting their work.

7.12 Social Media Engagement

1. Activism and Awareness: Erivo uses social media platforms to connect with fans, share her artistic journey, and effectively raise awareness about social issues. Her ability to interact directly with her audience enables her to sway public opinion and galvanize support for a range of causes.

2. Amplification of Voices: She frequently uses her platform to draw attention to the work of other activists, artists, and organizations, giving voices that might not otherwise be heard a chance to be heard.

7.13 Motivational Leader

1. Resilience and Determination: Many find inspiration in Erivo's narrative of overcoming adversity, which includes her experience in the cutthroat entertainment industry. Her will to succeed in a field dominated by white people inspires others to keep going and overcome obstacles.

2. Mentorship and Support: Erivo supports emerging artists and advocates for initiatives that promote diversity and inclusion in the arts, providing guidance and encouragement to those seeking to follow in her footsteps.

Cynthia Erivo's influence as an artist and advocate is significant and multifaceted. Through her performances, activism, and engagement with important social issues, she inspires change, challenges stereotypes, and empowers individuals to embrace their identities. As she continues to evolve in her career, her impact is likely to resonate across generations, solidifying her legacy as a transformative figure in both the entertainment industry and the realm of social justice.

CHAPTER 8: FUTURE PROJECTS AND ENDEAVORS

Cynthia Erivo is showcasing her talent and versatility in several exciting upcoming film, theater, and music projects. Here's a preview of what we can anticipate from her soon:

8.1 New Film Initiatives

1. Talent Show (TBA): Erivo and Anna Kendrick will feature in this upcoming movie. Because of the star

power of its leads, the movie is making waves despite the lack of details regarding the plot and her character.

2. The Color Purple (2023): Erivo leads this musical retelling of the classic 1985 film, which is also based on Alice Walker's novel. She performs as Celie, a role she played in the Broadway revival on stage earlier. Excitedly awaited, the movie will have a diverse cast, including Fantasia Barrino and Danielle Brooks.

3. Bounty (TBA): This action-thriller movie is currently in production and will also feature Erivo. There are currently no confirmed details about her character or the plot.

8.2 Future Projects in Theater

1. Broadway Return: Erivo is anticipated to make a comeback to the stage in a brand-new theatrical production, following her triumph in Broadway productions. Fans are excited to see her go back to her musical theater roots, even though specifics are still unknown.

8.3. Future Musical Initiatives

1. New Album: Erivo has made indications that she is working on new music, possibly a sequel to *Ella Mai*, her debut album. While exact information regarding the album's release date and track listing is still pending,

fans are thrilled about the possibility of hearing new songs that highlight her vocal prowess and songwriting abilities.

2. Collaborations: Erivo has indicated a desire to work with musicians from a variety of genres. Because of her musical versatility, she can experiment with various styles, and her fans can anticipate future projects that showcase her breadth of artistic expression.

8.4 Additional Creative Projects

1. Documentary Work: Erivo has indicated an interest in producing documentaries on social issues, with a focus on representation and racial justice. This could be a

fascinating addition to her body of work, even though details are still being worked out.

8.5 Potential production and directing roles

Beyond just acting and singing, Cynthia Erivo is a multifaceted talent who can also contribute significantly as a director and producer. Although specific projects are still being discussed, the following are some avenues and possibilities where she might explore directorial and production work:

8.6 Directorial Projects

Cynthia Erivo

1. Musical Adaptations: With her experience in musical theater, Erivo could direct stage productions of well-known musicals or her compositions. She could contribute her distinct perspective and grasp of performance to initiatives that emphasize strong storytelling and a variety of narratives.

2. Biographical Films: Erivo's portrayal of Harriet Tubman demonstrates her affinity for biographical stories. She might look into helming movies that chronicle the lives of other significant historical figures, especially those who came from underrepresented groups. Her unique perspectives could give these initiatives more substance and genuineness.

3. Social Justice Documentaries: Given her dedication to activism, Erivo could serve as director of films addressing social concerns like mental health, gender representation, or racial inequality. This would enable her to use her platform to tell powerful stories that inspire change and raise awareness.

4. Short Films and Series: Erivo may decide to make a series or a short film that addresses issues of community, empowerment, and identity. These initiatives might provide a platform for up-and-coming artists and a variety of viewpoints within the sector.

8.7 Manufacturing Activities

Cynthia Erivo

1. Production Company: Erivo could launch her own production business with the goal of creating and distributing media that highlights the experiences and voices of underrepresented people. Her control over the kinds of projects she supports and brings to life would increase as a result of this endeavor.

2. Collaborative Projects: Erivo may create theater plays, television shows, or films that reflect her ideals by teaming up with seasoned production companies or other artists. Creative and significant projects that connect with viewers could result from this partnership.

3. Music Production: As a musician, Erivo might look into opportunities in this field, collaborating with other musicians to make records that honor diversity and use

songs to tell stories. Her background in the field puts her in a good position to advise and assist up-and-coming talent.

8.8 Emphasis Areas and Themes

1. Empowerment and Resilience: Social justice, resilience, and empowerment are likely to be major themes in any project that Erivo directs or produces. Her commitment to elevating underrepresented voices may influence the stories she decides to share.

2. Cultural Representation: It is anticipated that Erivo will highlight the value of sharing diverse stories and cultural representation in his work. She might try to

create content that highlights the diversity of backgrounds and cultures.

8.9 Possible Partnerships

1. Established Filmmakers and Writers: Erivo is open to working with seasoned pros who appreciate the same kind of narrative. These collaborations may result in creative endeavors that fuse her artistic abilities with the know-how of seasoned pros.

2. Other Artists and Activists: Because of her considerable network in the entertainment sector, Erivo could collaborate with other artists and activists to

develop significant projects that tackle urgent social concerns.

CONCLUSION

Cynthia Erivo's career is proof of her extraordinary gift, tenacity, and dedication to narrative. Erivo has continuously shown her adaptability and love for the arts, from her start in theater to her ascent to prominence in music and film. Here is a summary of the salient features of her varied career:

Theater Breakthrough:
Erivo initially became well-known for her stirring performances in musical theater. She won a Tony Award for her performance as Celie in the Broadway production

of *The Color Purple*, solidifying her reputation as a formidable performer. Her success in music and film came from her ability to use songs to connect with audiences and express intense emotion.

Shift to Cinema:

Erivo has made an amazing move from stage to screen. Her portrayal of Harriet Tubman in the movie *Harriet* demonstrated her range as an actor and brought her praise from critics as well as numerous nominations for awards, including Best Actress and Best Original Song for the Academy Awards. Her talent was brought to light in this role, which also served as confirmation of her dedication to representing important historical figures and tales with social justice undertones.

. Achievements in Music:

Cynthia Erivo

Erivo's incredible vocal ability and depth of feeling have defined her musical career. Her ability to cross genres was demonstrated on her debut album, Ella Mai and her success as a musician was further cemented with the release of her single "Stand Up" from Harriet . Her music frequently resonates with listeners and motivates them to take action by highlighting themes of social justice, empowerment, and resilience.

Activism and Advocacy:

In addition to her artistic accomplishments, Erivo is a vocal supporter of social justice and diversity in the arts. She makes use of her position to speak out on important topics like women's rights, LGBTQ+ representation, and racial inequality. Her commitment to making a difference outside of the entertainment industry is demonstrated by her active participation in movements and her use of voice to advocate for change.

Influence on Culture:

Erivo makes a major contribution to the cultural discourse on history, race, and identity through his work. She dispels myths and promotes understanding by teaching audiences about the struggles faced by underrepresented groups via her performances. Her cultural impact is further amplified by her celebration of her Nigerian heritage and dedication to authentic representation.

Prospective Prospects:

Erivo has a wealth of exciting project possibilities ahead of her as a producer and director as her career develops. Her commitment to elevating underrepresented voices

Cynthia Erivo

and presenting thought-provoking tales makes it seem likely that she will make major and influential contributions to the field going forward.

Cynthia Erivo's remarkable talent, tenacity, and commitment to social justice have defined her varied career. She epitomizes the spirit of an artist who uses her platform to uplift and inspire, as seen by her stirring performances on stage and her influential roles in movies and music. Her story inspires both advocates and aspiring artists, showing that anyone can have a significant impact on the world if they are genuine, passionate, and determined. As she carries on break down barriers and question conventions; Erivo's legacy will surely continue to influence future generations.

www.ingramcontent.com/pod-product-compliance
Lightning Source LLC
Chambersburg PA
CBHW070358230526
45471CB00006B/2625